LETTER OF THE GREEKS
TO INNOCENT III

Thomas Morosini

Latin Patriarch of Jerusalem

Translated by: D.P. Curtin

Copyright @ 2020 Dalcassian Press

All rights reserved. No part of this publication may be reproduced, distributed, or transmitted in any form or by any means, including photocopying, recording, or other electronic or mechanical methods, without the prior written permission of the publisher, except in the case of brief quotations embodied in critical reviews and certain other non-commercial uses permitted by copyright law. For permission request, write to Dalcassian Press at dalcassianpublishing at gmail.com

ISBN: 979-8-3302-3449-3 (Paperback)

Library of Congress Control Number:
Author: Curtin, D.P. (1985-)

Printed by Ingram Content Group, 1 Ingram Blvd, La Vergne, Tennessee

First printing edition 2020.

LETTER OF THE GREEKS

LETTER OF THE GREEKS

Constantinopel

LETTER OF THE GREEKS TO INNOCENT III
After the Fall of Constantinople to the Latins, during the reign of the Emperor Henry

Lord, if we did not know that the present life is the eve of the divine Sabbath of the future, we would have composed a mournful tragedy to you, and with long lamentations we would have bewailed the captivity of the new people. But because we truly believe that Christ, who is always present with us, will transform this mortal life of ours into that immortal and more excellent life; behold, we rejoice, being contrite for the betterment, but also give thanks to Christ himself, who is with us, and again was willing to suffer for us. For he did not consider it robbery to be worshiped equally with God and the Father; rather, he was willingly handed over again; and being captured with us, he was stripped, abducted, and betrayed, and his body and blood were thrown to the ground and poured out, and trampled upon; and he endured all things, so that he might unite two peoples, killing enmities, or rather joining and uniting his own body torn in two back into one: "Who is wise, and will keep these things? Who is suitable," and will admire the divine providence towards us? Then it is sweet for us to have been captured, sweet to suffer, to be led into captivity, dear and pleasing. For in what way could we have made peace with our brothers, with whom we could not even bear to speak before? But are not the things that have been done against us serious? Certainly very serious, as they have indeed shaken the souls of the Latins, and the bodies of the

Romans or Greeks. But whoever has looked into the divine mysteries will see the judgments of God, and will behold the immense abyss. Many patriarchs and emperors have desired to see this day, but they have not obtained this grace.

You, Lord, after many generations, are united by this grace, and become the thirteenth apostle. And you know, honorable Lord, what sense has been given to men by God, and what the will of those who let the sacred bond of piety not be subjected to tyrannical force. For if it were not so, we would also baptize the Jews against their will. Therefore, it is absurd to impose punishment and coercion in matters of doctrine, for it is easy to do so, and belongs to anyone with power; on the other hand, persuading people by using the principles of doctrines is the work of a good man who seeks the truth. Will you, sir, choose to use force on us without examination, like brute animals, to change us, or rather allow our words and reasoning to be heard, and impart to us the reason and speech by which the truth of divine matters may be examined and known? For you should know that we will later prove and investigate what has been divinely handed down to us: "Search the Scriptures." None of us can be captured by violence, but we will all be in danger as if for Christ. Moreover, we think very probably that your spirit of wisdom will rightfully praise us in this matter. Praiseworthy is anyone who appeals to the judgment of a synod and the sentence that proceeds from there.

Therefore, since there is a small gap between the Latins and the Greeks, which has disrupted the unity of one Church, establish an ecumenical synod to be convened, and send vicars of your majesty with incense, and let there be a discussion and resolution of all controversies. If you also, following the great apostle Paul, are a helper of God, we are ready, my lord, to depart from the Constantinopolitan diocese, and undertake migration to the East or West. But we also believe to have our most excellent emperor as our lord, and to live under his protection, serving for wages, cultivating fields, feeding, sailing the sea: but without us the land will not be filled, nor the winepress, bread will not be eaten, nor meat, nor fish, nor vegetables; and neither will life and human interaction stand. And indeed, we labor for our Latin brothers, and we offer, from the worst part of our life, that which is mortal and must be dissolved; but we also desire to think the same according to the better, both while we live and after death, as members of one immortal body and therefore we write daily to our Western brothers in the region, fellow ministers and bishops, ready to gather in Constantinople. Indeed, wherever we are located in any province, we suggest that in place of the deceased pontiffs, others be ordained according to the canons; especially above all, in the royal city. For it is necessary for everyone to sit in the synod, both our patriarch, metropolitans, and other pontiffs, and nothing mutilated or imperfect will be found among us.

But we also need the patriarch of the same opinion and voice before the synod, who will teach. Let him undertake and exercise his customary functions, and receive our confessions. For this reason, in Jerusalem and Antioch, when there was one king, there were two popes, one Roman, the other Latin, of the same opinion and language as them, and still very similar to them. For it is not right for anyone to confess hidden matters through an interpreter in the language of another patriarch, even if there may be agreement in opinions. Therefore, these things should be observed up to the point of union with us. For we wish and desire that they once again possess apostolic authority, synodically, imperial laws and constitutions, inasmuch as they decree that the pontiffs of each province should be elected and ordained from the beginning of the same province. We also request from your pontifical magnificence that you accept this present letter of our humility, and that you may wish to convene a general synod, in which the truth of divine dogmas may be judged. Since it is impossible for both sides to be in the right opinion; because things that are contrary are not the same. For by geometric necessity, one finds the lowest cornerstone, the connector of the oblique, and there exists a right angle, which admits neither greater nor lesser. For if it is changed to greater, it will be obtuse, and if to lesser, acute; and both of these are indefinite.

However, since our emperor, promoted by God and a devoted follower of Christ, has commanded us to show proper respect to his highness

LETTER OF THE GREEKS

with goodwill, we have respected his edict of mercy and have decided to bestow upon you, lord, the appropriate honor, which is praise and acclaim equal to imperial praises and acclamations, as follows: "To Innocent, lord and pope of ancient Rome, many years." This should be proclaimed by us after the final prayer of the gathering, until the Holy Spirit council convenes us and leads us to a perfect understanding of sacred doctrine. For then, with bare heads, from the pulpit, amidst the sacred offering itself, not only we, but also Ethiopians, Libyans, Egyptians, Syrians, Russians, Alans, Goths, Iberians, and all peoples subject to our teachings, will proclaim your name; and Christ himself will inscribe it before all in the holy books; he who bears witness to us that we do not desire to conquer, but rather to rejoice as the conquered should, as long as we have seen the light. For whoever in this life is not cautious and safe regarding doctrines will suffer loss in death, receiving fire and darkness as inheritance, because he did not recognize the light. Therefore, with this loss presupposed, and having mercy on the many thousands of perishing people, we write to your holiness in the Holy Spirit with exclamation, so that you may quickly arrange for a universal council to be convened, for the benefit of Christians and for the salvation of your holy soul.

LATIN TEXT

LETTER OF THE GREEKS

Domine, nisi sciremus præsentem vitam esse futuri divini Sabbati Parasceven, lugubrem ad te tragediam concinnassemus, longisque lamentationibus novi populi captivitatem deflevissemus. Quia vero bene credidimus. Christum, qui nobis semper adsistit, mortalem hanc nostram vitam ad immortalem illam et præstantiorem transformare; ecce contriti, propter reformationem in melius, lætamur; sed et agimus gratias ipsi Christo, qui nobiscum est, iterumque pro nobis pati voluit. Non enim rapinam arbitratus est adorari æqualiter cum Deo et Patre; verum iterum sponte traditus est; et nobiscum captus, spoliatus est', abductus ac proditus, ipsiusque corpus et sanguinem in terram dejecerunt ac effuderunt, atque conculcaverunt; necnon cuncta sustinuit, ut duos populos connecteret, interficiens inimicitias, seu potius corpus suum in duo scissum rursus in unum conjungeret et adunaret: "Quis sapiens, et custodiet hæc? Quis idoneus," et divinam erga nos providentiam admirabitur? Dehinc nobis dulce est captos fuisse, suave pati, in captivitatem duci carum et gratum. Quo enim modo cum fratribus nostris unionem fecissemus, cum quibus ne vel colloqui antea sustinebamus? Sed gravia sunt quæ adversus nos acta fuere? Profecto plane gravia, ut quæ Latinorum quidem animas, Romanorum vero seu Græcorum corpora labefactarint. Verum qui in divina secreta introspexerit, judicia Dei, immensam abyssum conspecturus est. Multi patriarche et imperatores diem hunc videre desideraverunt, sed eam gratiam non sunt consecuti. Tu, domine, post multas generationes hac gratia unias, et decimus tertius apostolus fias ac Nosti autem, honorande domine, quis sensus hominibus a Deo datus fuerit, quodque volentium, non tyrannicam vim passorum sit pietatis sacramentum. Hoc enim si ita non esset, ipsos quoque Judæos baptizaremus invitos. Quia igitur in dogmatibus poenam quidem irrogare et cogere absurdum est, facillimum quippe, ac potentis cujuslibet; persuadere autem, dogmatum principiis utendo, boni viri est et colentis veritatem; electurusne es, domine, nobis vim absque examine adhibere, tanquam brutis animantibus, ut mutemur, an potius sermones nostros admittere, et rationem orationemque nobis impertiri, quo divinarum rerum veritas expendatur et cognoscatur. Scito namque, a nobis posterius probari et quæri, quod illi divinitus tradito verbo obtemperemus: Scrutamini Scripturas. Per violentiam autem nemo nostrum capi potest; sed cuncti quasi pro Christo periclitabimur. Porro existimamus admodum verisimiliter, spiritum sapientice tue jure merito nos ea in re laudaturum. Laudabilis enim est quicumque ad synodicum judicium, illincque procedentem sententiam appellat.

Itaque quandoquidem exiguum interstitium Latinos inter et Græcos est, quod unius Ecclesiæ continuitatem solvit, statue synodum cecumenicam congregari, et majestatis ture vicarios mittito, fiatque colloquium, omniumque controversorum solutio. Si tu quoque, juxta magnum apostolum Paulum, Dei fueris adjutor, prompti sumus, domine, nos quoque a dicecesi Constantinopolitana discedere, atque migrationem in Orientem vel Occidentem suscipere. Sed et putamus dominum habere imperatorem nostrum Sirerrim, atque sub ejus umbra vivere, mercede servire, agros colere, pascere, mare navigare: absque nobis autem non implebitur area, neque torcular, non comedetur panis, non caro, non piscis, non olus; sed nec stabit vita et conversatio humana. Et hæc quidem elaboramus fratribus nostris Latinis, atque conferimus, ex deteriori vite nostræ portione, mortali nimirum illa et dissolvenda; cupimus autem etiam juxta potiorem eadem sentire, tum quandiu vivimus, tum post mortem, ut qui membra simus unius corporis immortalis ideoque scribimus quotidie ad Occidentales per regionem fratres nostros, comministros et coepiscopos, paratos esse ad Constantinopolim convenire. Quin etiam in quacumque provincia positis suggerimus, ut in locum defunctorum pontificum, alios juxta canonum præscripta ordinent; maximeque præ omnibus, in urbe regia. Oportet enim cunctos in synodo considere, tum nostrum patriarcham, tum metropolitas, aliosque pontifices, nihilque mutilum imperfectumque inveniri apud nos.

Opus autem nobis est etiam ante synodum patriarcha ejusdem sententiæ ac vocis, qui doceat Consueta et impertiat, nostrasque suscipiat confessiones. Eapropter namque Hierosolymis et Antiochiæ, cum unus rex esset, duo erant pontifices, Romæis, alter, alter Latinis, ejusdem cum iis opinionis et linguæ, adhucque ipsis consimilis. Neque enim fas est ut quispiam per interpretem occulta confiteatur patriarchæ alterius linguæ, quamvis forsan sententiarum consensus adsit. Oportet igitur hæc usque ad unionem erga nos observari quoque. Volumus siquidem et optamus, ut iterum sua auctoritate potiantur apostolica, synodicæ, imperatorum legumque constitutiones, quatenus præcipiunt uniuscujusque provinciæ pontifices a primo ejusdem provinciæ eligi atque ordinari. Petimus etiam a tua pontificali magnificentia, ut præsens tenuitatis nostræ epistolium admittat, velitque synodum generalem cogi, quo divinorum dogmatum veritas dijudicetur. Cum fieri nequeat utramque partem in vera esse sententia; quoniam quæ contraria sunt, non sunt eadem. Geometrica enim necessitate unus invenitur lapis imus angularis, obliquorum connexor, unusque exsistit rectus angulus, qui neque majus neque minus admittit. Siquidem in majus mutatus, erit obtusus, in minus vero, acutus; atque horum uterque indefinitus.

Caeterum quoniam a Deo promotus et Christi studiosus imperator noster precepit nobis, ut convenientem honorem celsitudini tum benevole tribuamus, reveriti sumus clementiae ejus edictum, et constituimus tibi, domine, congruum honorem deferre, qui est laudatio et acclamatio imperatoriis laudibus acclamationibusque aequalis, ita ad verbum: "Innocentii domini papae veteris Romae, multos annos;" quae a nobis proferri debeat post ultimam collectarum orationem; donec Spiritus sanctum concilium coegerit, nosque ad sacri dogmatis perfectam duxerit cognitionem. Tunc enim nudo capite, ex ambone, inter ipsam sacram oblationem, non solum nos, sed Ethiopes simul ac Libyes, Egyptii et Syri, Russi, Alani, Gotthi, Iberi, omnesque gentes quae doctrinae nostrae subjiciuntur, tuum nomen proclamabunt; necnon ante cunctos ipse Christus sanctis libris inscribet; qui nobis testis sit, quod vincere non gestiamus, sed prout oportet victi, gavisuri simus; dummodo lucem conspexerimus. Nam qui in hacce vita erga dogmata cautus tutusque non est, damnum in morte feret, ignem ac tenebras in haereditatem accepturus, pro eo quod lumen non agnoverit. Hoc nos igitur damno praesupposito, multaque hominum pereuntium dena millia miserati, ad sanctitatem tuam in sancto Spiritu cum exclamatio scribimus; ut citius universale concilium congregari cures, ad utilitatem Christianorum, sanctaeque animae tuae salutem.

LETTER OF THE GREEKS

The Scriptorium Project is the work of a small group of lay people of various apostolic churches who are interested in the preservation, transmission, and translation of the works of the early and medieval church. Our efforts are to make the works of the church fathers accessible to anyone who might have an interest in Christian antiquities and the theological, philosophical, and moral writings that have become the bedrock of Western Civilization.

To-date, our releases have pulled from the Greek, Syriac, Georgian, Latin, Celtic, Ethiopian, and Coptic traditions of Christianity, and have been pulled from sundry local traditions and languages.

LETTER OF THE GREEKS

LETTER OF THE GREEKS

LETTER OF THE GREEKS

www.ingramcontent.com/pod-product-compliance
Lightning Source LLC
LaVergne TN
LVHW061044070526
838201LV00073B/5181